Amazing Encounters with the Living God
You Can Have Them, Too!

Lizbeth A. Diamond

DEDICATION

This book is dedicated to our heavenly Father, Creator of heaven and earth, the Eternal God, Yahweh;

and to His only begotten Son, Jesus Christ our Lord, Savior, Redeemer, the Way, the Truth and the Life, Soon and Coming King, Yeshua;

and to the precious Holy Spirit, our Teacher, Helper and Comforter, Ruach Hakodesh.

CONTENTS

INTRODUCTION

One day in prayer the Lord said to me, "I want you to write a book". "A book about what?" I asked. "About your experiences and encounters with Me."

Actually, He said the words experiences and encounters at that same time. I've noticed that He speaks that way sometimes, saying two or more words simultaneously.

Here's my prayer for you:

Father, bless the reader of this book. Reveal yourself to them, draw them into a deeper relationship with you and give them even greater experiences and encounters with you, in Jesus name. Amen.

CHAPTER 1

THE SIMPLE TRUTH

In March of 1990, things looked hopeless. I had big problems in every area of my life. I had hit rock bottom and was just in complete despair.

It was Good Friday, although I didn't realize it at the time that I cried out to the Lord for help. I had stepped outside at work to smoke a cigarette. I wasn't even sure that God existed, but I prayed, "God, I don't know if you're real or not, but if you are real, please help me. I just can't make it on my own. Please give me what I need." Well, He answered my prayer that same day!

That afternoon I had so much work to do that I didn't go to lunch until about two o'clock. I went down the street to Campbell's Bar-B-Que, expecting it to be empty at that time of day. Instead, it was packed. When I walked in there was a man standing at the counter, who had just placed his order and we said hello to each other. Now, I didn't know it at the time, but this restaurant is owned and run by a preacher.

The employees are very outgoing and loud. They ask for

your name when you order and when this man's food was ready they said, "Jeff, your sandwich is ready," and then yelled out into the restaurant, "Jeff needs a place to sit."

Well, two girls got up from their table and said, "We're done. He can have our table." So, he went over and sat down and I'm thinking, "Oh, no! My order will be ready next."

Sure enough, they announced loudly, "Liz, your sandwich is ready" and "Jeff, Liz is coming over to share your table." I felt like I had no choice but to walk over and share a table with some guy I didn't know, at a time when I really didn't want any company.

We started talking, just small talk at first. I had some books with me on divorce and explaining divorce to children and I was troubled. Jeff brought up the subject of God. I said that I had been looking for a church to take my children to, since they had been asking questions that I couldn't answer, but that I didn't really want to go back to the Catholic Church. First he suggested I go to a Church of God nearby, which I half-heartedly said I would check out. Truthfully, it was not a priority at the time. Then he said, "Actually, I am a pastor and I have my own church."

Those words pierced my heart! At once, I remembered my prayer of that morning and knew that this was an answer to that prayer. I was astonished! Not only was my prayer answered, but this meant that God did exist and He had some kind of incredible power to be able to orchestrate this meeting! I thought back on the events of that day, crying out to God in the morning, going to lunch later in the day than I ever had, the crowd at the restaurant when it should have been nearly empty, the way the employees had seated us together with no way to back out, and now this! A pastor! I was speechless.

Jeff gave me directions to Jubilee Church and told me that he had been saved 10 years ago almost to the day. I barely heard him. I knew that I would be coming to his church and somehow I knew that I would be coming to the Lord.

Well, my first Sunday at Jubilee Church was Easter Sunday! That was the day that I heard the truth for the first time in my life. That Jesus Christ is Lord, that He is the Son of God, that He lived on this earth, died for my sins and rose again on the third day that I might have eternal life. And all I had to do was pray a simple prayer to ask for forgiveness for my sins and to invite Jesus into my heart. Now I was saved! Born again! Became a child of God! It was truly the most wonderful day of my life!

The simple truth is that God loves you and He has a great plan for your life!

Do you know for sure that you will go to heaven?

You can know for sure. The Bible tells us how. *"We have all sinned and fallen short of the glory of God,"* and, *"the wages of sin is death, but the free gift of God is eternal life through Jesus Christ our Lord."* and, *"Whoever calls upon the name of the Lord will be saved."*

It's so simple! If you would like to receive the free gift that God has for you, eternal life through Jesus Christ and know for sure that you will go to heaven when you die, pray the following prayer out loud and believe it in your heart:

Dear Lord Jesus, come into my heart. Forgive me of all my sin. Wash me and cleanse me. Set me free. Jesus, thank you that you died for me. I believe that you have risen from the dead and that you're coming back for me. Fill me with your Holy Spirit. I'm saved, I'm forgiven and I'm on my way to heaven because I have Jesus in my heart. Amen.

If you prayed that simple prayer, God heard you and has forgiven all of your sins. You have become a born again child of God, old things are passed away and all things are new.

SOWING SEED

Later on I realized that the Lord had sent three different people to me to help lead me to Him.

First, it was an old friend and his girlfriend who I heard had gotten saved in Australia. I wasn't sure what saved meant, but they came to me at a pool party and started talking to me about God. I ignored them and was even kind of rude to them because I thought they had gone off the deep end.

Then, one day at work at a temporary job I listened as a couple of co-workers talked about God. After a while one of them asked me what I believed. Earlier, I had decided that I was an agnostic and believed that there might be a God, but if there was He didn't want us to know Him. However, when I was asked what I believed, suddenly my mind went completely blank on the subject. I thought that was very strange.

Finally, after work one day, another co-worker asked me for a ride to the bank to cash her paycheck. As we drove along, she would say things like, "Thank you, Jesus!" in response to something good happening. It seemed like maybe there was something to this whole Jesus thing, because I could actually see good things happening to her.

Shortly after these events was when I cried out to God. I never saw any of those people again, although I often wanted to thank them for being bold enough to witness to me. I believe they planted seeds in my heart.

"What, after all, is Apollos? And what is Paul? Only <u>servants, through whom you came to believe—as the Lord has assigned to each his task</u>. I planted the seed, Apollos watered it, but God has been making it grow. So neither the one who plants nor the one who waters is anything, but only God, who makes things grow. <u>The one who plants and the one who waters have one purpose, and they will each be rewarded according to their own labor</u>." 1 Corinthians 3: 5-9 NIV

"The sower sows the word." Mark 4:14

This taught me an important lesson about witnessing and speaking God's word to the unsaved. You might never see the results, but God will bring in His harvest.

THE POWER OF PRAYER

Several months later, I met a lady at church who said that about a year ago the Lord had directed her to pray over our entire area for unsaved people. I felt in my heart that God had answered her prayer in part by sending people to me and then saving me. He does answer prayer, even though we might not see it right away.

Years later I started hearing stories about how Jesus was appearing to Muslims in dreams and they were giving their hearts to Him and getting saved.

I asked the Lord why He didn't send someone to witness to me or appear to me Himself earlier in my life. It would have saved me years of heartache, walking in darkness. His answer shocked me! He said, "No one prayed for you."

Wow! It's so important that we pray for the unsaved.

"Therefore said he unto them, The harvest truly is great, but the laborers are few: pray ye therefore the Lord of the harvest, that he would send forth laborers into his harvest." Luke 10:2

"But I say unto you, Love your enemies, bless them that curse you, do good to them that hate you, and pray for them which despitefully use you, and persecute you." Matthew 5:44

"In whom the god of this world hath blinded the minds of them which believe not, lest the light of the glorious gospel of Christ, who is the image of God, should shine unto them." 2 Corinthians 4:4

The Bible tells us that the god of this world, Satan, has blinded the minds of the unsaved to try to keep them from receiving the good news of the gospel. But, Jesus has given us authority over Satan and commissioned us to preach the gospel and see people set free! Hallelujah!

CHAPTER 2

THERE'S NO HIGH LIKE THE MOST HIGH

When I first began to learn how to worship God, the most amazing peace I've ever felt came over me. All of my problems seemed to disappear as I became aware only of the presence of God.

The pastor read to us where the bible says, *"Lift up your hands in the sanctuary and praise the Lord."* Psalm 134:2

He said to close your eyes, lift your hands, forget about everyone around you and focus on the Lord.

The band started playing and we all started singing the worship song. It was so hard to lift my hands at first. I felt so self-conscious, like everyone was looking at me and judging me, but I did it anyway and oh, the peace and joy that came over me!

I remember thinking that this was a feeling that no drugs or alcohol can give. No hangover and completely free of charge. Just perfect peace, love and complete well being. There's no high like the Most High God.

As I continued to press in to God, there were times when He would speak to me during worship. I didn't hear Him with my ears, I heard Him inside my heart. His words are very powerful! There were other times where I could actually see Him. I didn't see Him with my natural eyes, my eyes were closed, but I could see Him with my spiritual eyes. He was seated on a throne and very awesome!

"God is spirit, and his worshippers must worship in the Spirit and in truth." John 4:24

I continued to learn the importance of being led by the spirit in worship. Sometimes He would lead me to raise my hands, sometimes to kneel, sometimes to dance. Whenever I followed His lead it always brought me into a deeper place in God's presence.

"For as many as are led by the Spirit of God, they are the sons of God." Romans 8:14

Once, I had injured my knee, was in a lot of pain and limped into church. We started worshiping. Somehow, in His presence, I forgot about my knee and I felt led to start dancing and spinning around. When worship ended, I took my seat and suddenly realized that all the pain was gone from my knee!

I tried to tell my family and friends about the truth that I had found, but they didn't seem to understand. I probably didn't explain it very well. I really wanted them to experience salvation and how great God is. I kept on inviting them and in particular, my brother Thomas to church.

One morning I was reading the Bible and these words just leapt off the page,"*And Thomas answered and said unto him, My Lord and my God.*" John 20:28

Later that same day, Thomas called me and said, "I have a favor to ask you. Could you babysit for us tonight? I know what you're going to say, you will if we come to church. Okay, we will."

Wow, I wasn't even thinking that. Well, Thomas and his wife came to church the next Sunday and heard the truth of the gospel. When an altar call was given, they both went up front and prayed a prayer to invite Jesus into their hearts. Thomas started pounding on his chest, and loudly saying, "I've never received anything like this! I've never received anything like this!" He cried tears of joy.

"Therefore if any man be in Christ, he is a new creature: old things are passed away; behold, all things are become new." 2 Corinthians 5:17

"And hope maketh not ashamed; because <u>the love of God is shed abroad in our hearts by the Holy Ghost</u> which is given unto us." Romans 5:5

"That if thou shalt confess with thy mouth the Lord Jesus, and shalt believe in thine heart that God hath raised him from the dead, thou shalt be saved. For with the heart man believeth unto righteousness; and with the mouth confession is made unto salvation." Romans 10: 9-10

CHAPTER 3

THE JOY OF THE LORD IS YOUR STRENGTH

I heard about a pastor named Rodney Howard-Browne who said that the Lord had sent him from his native country of South Africa to the United States as a missionary. I thought that was odd, because usually people from the U.S. go to other countries as missionaries. I heard that during Rodney Howard-Browne's meetings people would get full of the joy of the Lord and start laughing. I wanted to go check it out, but some people at the church I was attending at that time warned me that it wasn't of the Lord and that he didn't teach the bible. I went anyway.

He was having a meeting in an arena in Tampa. As he took to the platform and began to speak, he read out loud two entire chapters of the bible! As I sat in my seat listening, I began to smell a fragrance like incense. It got stronger and stronger and I started looking around at the people nearby to see if someone was burning incense. Then, I looked up at the vents on the ceiling to see if they were piping incense in, but I didn't see any smoke coming out. The lady next to me noticed me looking around and so I asked her if she smelled anything like incense burning. She said, "No, I think that's just for you."

That's when I found out that you can supernaturally smell things in the spirit, that Rodney Howard-Browne does teach and preach out of the bible and that other Christians don't always know what they're talking about.

I attended several more meetings, and then spent the next 3 years as a member of The River at Tampa Bay, Rodney Howard-Browne's church, full of joy, laughing, falling on the floor and being touched and changed by the spirit of God in a major way. I continued to discover that God is not boring, dry or religious and no matter how hard I try, I can't totally figure Him out.

"Then was our mouth filled with laughter, and our tongue with singing: then said they among the heathen, The Lord hath done great things for them." Psalm 126:2

"Thou wilt shew me the path of life: in thy presence is fulness of joy; at thy right hand there are pleasures for evermore." Psalm 16:11

"And when I saw him, I fell at his feet as dead. And he laid his right hand upon me, saying unto me, Fear not; I am the first and the last" Revelation 1:17

A LAUGHING STOCK

Years later, in another church, the lady next to me and I got filled with the joy of the Lord and started laughing in our seats. The Lord said to me, "I'm going to make you a spectacle. I'm going to make you a laughing stock." I was so joyful that I didn't even consider His words in the moment.

Then we had communion. Everyone was supposed to go to the front in a line and two people were standing up there with the bread and wine. It was the first time I ever had communion at that church and I was one of the first people up there because I was sitting near the front. I went to the first person and took a communion wafer and ate it. Then I went to the second person and saw that they were holding a cup of wine that I was supposed to dip my wafer in. I realized I had done it wrong and just let out a little laugh at how dumb I was. Suddenly, the joy of the Lord hit me really hard and I fell down laughing and couldn't move. I was lying on my side and it started to get really uncomfortable and I remember thinking, "If only I could just move my leg a little bit, it would feel a lot better," but I couldn't move anything at all. The rest of the church filed past me as they took communion and it was like waves of joy kept washing over me as laughter ebbed and flowed.

Afterwards, I thought back on what the Lord had said, "I'm going to make you a spectacle. I'm going to make you a laughing stock." I was amazed at his terminology! I was laughing on the floor and I assumed it was a spectacle to those other church goers.

"The Lord is my shepherd; I shall not want. He maketh me to lie down in green pastures: he leadeth me beside the still waters." Psalm 23:2

"for we are made a spectacle unto the world, and to angels, and to men. We are fools for Christ's sake, but ye are wise in Christ; we are weak, but ye are strong; ye are honorable, but we are despised."   1 Corinthians 4:9-11

"Whom having not seen, ye love; in whom, though now ye see him not, yet believing, ye <u>rejoice with joy unspeakable and full of glory.</u>" 1 Peter 1:8

Here's my prayer for you:

Father, fill the reader of this book with Your joy unspeakable and full of glory, in Jesus name. Amen.

CHAPTER 4

DON'T LET THE HARVEST ROT IN THE FIELD

One day at work I started to smell something that smelled like rotting oranges. I looked all around the office and even in my bosses trash can, thinking maybe he ate an orange and left the peels in there for a really long time. I couldn't find the source of the smell. I went home after work and started to smell that same odor, like rotting oranges. I looked all around my apartment and didn't find the source of the smell. It seemed strange that I would smell that both at work and at home.

Finally, I asked the Lord, "What is that smell?" He said, "Don't let the harvest rot in the field. Don't let the harvest rot." I knew what He meant because He had been dealing with me go out and witness to people.

I had a map of Tampa and in praying over it the Lord said, "Pick 3 zip codes." I circled 3 zip codes on the map and stepped out to reach souls there. I quit my job and for the next 3 months focused on sharing the gospel with the people in those 3 zip codes. My partner and I had requested boxes of Christian magazines be donated to us from the publisher. We also bought a large amount of gospel tracts. We rolled a magazine and rubber banded a gospel tract to it. Then, we loaded these into bags in the back seat of my car.

Starting at the first zip code, which happened to be a lower income, higher crime area of Tampa that we affectionately referred to as the Hood, I drove my Lincoln Mark IV up and down every street, throwing a magazine into each driveway. When we saw a person outside, we pulled up to give them a free magazine and preached the gospel to them. Without fail, as soon as the first person prayed to receive Jesus, every other person we talked to that day also said a prayer of salvation. It was awesome!

One day we were talking with a small group that had gathered around the car. I saw a man fling open the front curtains in his house, look at us with wide open eyes and come running to the car to get saved. It was supernatural. Jesus said, "If I be lifted up, I will draw all men to me." We experienced that again and again, we started out talking with one person and then the Spirit of God would draw a crowd of people to us.

By summer's end, 300 people had prayed to receive Jesus. That's 300 people in 3 months in 3 zip codes! It was like God put His signature on the whole outreach.

Then, my children and I were about to be evicted from our apartment for not being able to pay the rent, so I scrambled to get another job. Season over.

TODAY IS THE DAY OF SALVATION

I did continue to go on soul winning street outreaches on the weekends with a group of like minded Christians. One day we met a lady on the street who asked us to come to the nursing home where she worked to pray for the residents there. It was a short walk down a side street and we went from room to room sharing the gospel with many people, and both residents and nursing home employees gave their hearts to Jesus.

I entered the room of one young man in particular. He was maybe in his early 30s, wearing a hospital gown and he looked very ill. I shared the gospel with him and he eagerly agreed to pray a prayer to receive Jesus as his savior. The joy of the Lord filled that man! When we came back to the nursing home the following week, we were told that he had passed away. It made me cry to think that his eternal destination had changed just in time. The Lord is so good!

"As God's co-workers we urge you not to receive God's grace in vain. For he says, "In the time of my favor I heard you, and in the day of salvation I helped you." I tell you, now is the time of God's favor, now is the day of salvation." 2 Corinthians 6:1-2 NIV

One weekend at the nursing home, I was out on the back patio talking to people about Jesus. A man who looked to be in his late 80's became very angry and started yelling at me and cursing Jesus. He couldn't speak very clearly, his words were slurred and I thought that maybe he had previously had a stroke. It caused quite a scene and the other people out there were watching and listening to his tirade. Then, the strangest thing happened. The peace of God came over me in such a strong way that as I stood before that man, I was completely unaffected by his words. I just looked at him in wonder and peace.

The following week, we came back to the nursing home and held a worship service for the residents. We did tag team preaching so that each of the 7 of us shared a brief message. Afterwards, we went out into the crowd to pray with each individual. I walked over to the man who had screamed at me the previous week and asked him how I could pray for him. He said to me in a perfectly clear voice, "Pray that Jesus would save me." I led him in a prayer of salvation and after he received Jesus, his entire face changed and he was filled with joy! Wow!

HE PREPARES A TABLE BEFORE YOU

At that time, I was working in an office with 2 women that were making my life miserable. They were as aggressively unkind to me as they could be and one lady in particular would get a little group of co-workers together and whisper about me, looking over at me with disdain on their faces. It was really unpleasant and went on for months.

I came in to work one morning which happened to be my birthday, walked back to my desk and was surprised and overwhelmed to see that another woman who worked in our office had decorated my cubicle to the max and there were presents all over my desk and chair. The Holy Spirit immediately spoke to me and said, "I prepare a table before you in the presence of your enemies." Wow! He's so good!

"Thou preparest a table before me in the presence of mine enemies: thou anointest my head with oil; my cup runneth over." Psalm 23:5

CHAPTER 5

THE POWER OF GOD

My daughter was dating a young man that I felt very uncomfortable about. He came by one day while she was gone and we sat together talking. I sensed in my spirit that there was some demonic presence and began to minister to him. I had some scriptures about deliverance and felt impressed to ask him to simply read them out loud and to make them personal. He started reading:

"Ye are of God, little children, and have overcome them: because greater is He that is in ME, than he that is in the world." 1 John 4:4

"For the weapons of our warfare are not carnal, but mighty through God to the pulling down of strong holds: casting down imaginations, and every high thing that exalts itself against the knowledge of God, and bringing into captivity every thought to the obedience of Christ." 2 Corinthians 10:4

"Behold I give you power to tread on serpents and scorpions, and over all the power of the enemy: and nothing shall by any means hurt ME." Luke 10:19

"But if I cast out devils by the Spirit of God, then the kingdom of God is come unto you. Or else how can one enter into a strong man's house, and spoil his goods, except he first bind the strong man? And then he will spoil his house. I bind the strong man in MY life in the Name of the Lord Jesus Christ." Matthew 16:28

That's as far as he got. He jumped up and ran into the bathroom. When he came out he told me that he had thrown up 5 objects that looked like round, black stones! He went free, rejoicing!

JUBILEE

My children, grandson and I were living in an apartment that was too small for all of us. I kept praying and asking the Lord for a bigger place. One night, I fell down on my knees and cried out to Him and I felt something break in the spirit. The next day, my son announced that he was moving out of state with his girlfriend to be near her mom and dad. I felt very grieved about being so far away from them and did an online job search in that town.

Amazingly, I found exactly the job I was qualified for at a large, well known company and with a much higher salary. I sent my resume and got a call back to schedule an interview. The company flew me up there, picked me up at the airport and we met for an interview. Then, my son took me to look at apartments and I found a large, beautiful, 3 bedroom for rent that I could easily afford.

A little while after I got back to town, they called to offer me the job which I accepted.

As we were packing the truck, the Lord spoke to me and said, "It's your Jubilee year." I was fifty years old!

"Consecrate the fiftieth year and proclaim liberty throughout the land to all its inhabitants. It shall be a jubilee for you; *each of you is to return to your family property and to your own clan."* Leviticus 25:10

FOLLOW AFTER PEACE

I was driving an older car and it started to have mechanical problems. I was stopped at a red light in heavy traffic when it stalled and wouldn't restart. I prayed for help! Then, I looked over to my right and there was an auto repair shop! So, I walked over, told them what happened and they pushed my car into the garage to repair it. Once I was back on the road I said to the Lord, "I really need a newer car." At once I had the thought to apply for a car loan at my credit union. That was an answer to prayer, because I'd never had a car loan or even thought of applying for one before. I got approved for a loan and went shopping for a car, but didn't have peace on buying any that I saw.

I went to church the next Sunday and after service my friend told me that the worship leader was a car salesman! I talked to him about it and said that I was leaning towards a Toyota Camry. "Great," he said, "I work at the Toyota dealership. I'll take a look at our inventory tomorrow and give you a call." He called the next day to say that he had just the right Camry for me, so I went in for a test drive and loved it. We had to wait for the finance manager to be available and I started telling the worship leader my story and that I didn't have peace on any of those other cars I'd seen. As we walked down the hallway to the finance office he said, "Yes, it's so important to follow after peace." We walked into the office and the worship leader introduced me to the finance manager. He said, "This is Biff Peace." I almost fell over! His last name was Peace!

"Through the tender mercy of our God; whereby the dayspring from on high hath visited us, To give light to them that sit in darkness and in the shadow of death, to guide our feet into the way of peace." Luke 1:78-80

SHARING THE GOSPEL

One day at work, a group of co-workers were gathered around my desk and we were talking. The boss came over and listened in for awhile which made us all uncomfortable, so everyone went back to their desks. Later, he came back and said in a very stern voice that he wanted to see me in his office. I figured I was in trouble and followed him back to his office. He said to close the door and sit down and I wondered if he was going to fire me.

Instead, he said, "I heard you say something about God out there and I wanted to ask you about it." Wow! I don't know what I had said, I wasn't trying to purposely say anything, it was just the Lord's doing. We talked for quite awhile, I shared the gospel with him and he gave his heart to Jesus!

"Preach the word; be instant in season, out of season; reprove, rebuke, exhort with all long suffering and doctrine." 2 Timothy 4:2

THE FIRE OF GOD

I went to a Tommy Tenney conference and at the end of the service, he asked all the full time ministers to come to the altar. He prayed over them, laid hands on them and then asked them to turn around and go pray for the rest of the congregation. A lady came up to me and she was visibly shaking under the power of God. She held my face in both of her hands and yelled, "Fire!" It was so powerful! I didn't just fall backwards; I was actually catapulted backwards and flew through the air about 2 feet off the ground. The catcher must have seen me flying toward him and freaked out and stepped aside, so I hit the floor with a bang and was out under the power of God for a couple of hours.

"For our God is a consuming fire." Hebrews 12:29

"John answered, saying unto them all, I indeed baptize you with water; but one mightier than I cometh, the latchet of whose shoes I am not worthy to unloose: <u>he shall baptize you with the Holy Ghost and with fire</u>" Luke 3:16

WHATEVER HE SAYS TO YOU, DO IT

I designed a soul winning Christmas card that I sent to family, friends and co-workers every year. It clearly shared the gospel and invited the reader to pray a prayer of salvation. Many people were touched by it and told me so.

One co-worker came into my office in tears saying, "Thank you for this card! This is exactly what I needed!" Another co-worker told me that she had been raised a Catholic and that this was the first time she had prayed to receive Jesus.

She was so happy!

Another co-worker of Oriental descent came to me to say thank you and said that even though she had been raised in another kind of religion, she found the words to be quite beautiful and very touching.

One year, the Lord showed me an organization that asks for donations of signed Christmas cards to be distributed to members of the military both here and abroad. It was a Red Cross program called Christmas Cards for Heroes. I felt impressed to print 1,000 soul winning cards, sign them and take them to their distribution center.

The following year in October, I smelled something burning. I looked all around my house to find the source of the smell, then went outside to check my neighbors' houses and yards, but couldn't find anything burning. I went to a worship meeting the following Saturday night and started to smell that same burning smell! It smelled like someone had lit a match only it was a lot stronger than that. Finally, I asked the Lord' "What is that smell?" He said, "It's souls burning in hell." Yikes! Okay, He had my attention now.

I asked Him what he wanted me to do. He said, "Make 10,000 Christmas cards." Wow! That was a lot of printing and signing, but He gave me the grace to do it. So, 10,000 soul winning Christmas cards were distributed to servicemen and women that year. Glory to God!

"His mother saith unto the servants, <u>Whatsoever he saith unto you, do it.</u>" John 2:5

"And <u>this gospel of the kingdom shall be preached in all the world for a witness unto all nations;</u> and then shall the end come." Matthew 24:14

CHAPTER 6

SEEING IN THE SPIRIT REALM

I heard about a teacher named Gary Oates who wrote a book called *Open My Eyes, Lord*. He teaches about how you can see into the spirit realm and that seeing in the spirit is for everyone. I went to his conference, read his book and I received an activation so that I started to see in the spirit in a way I never had before. I had seen brief visions of God and Jesus seated on their thrones during worship, but now the spirit realm really opened up to me.

"Then Elisha prayed and said, "O Lord, I pray, <u>open his eyes</u> <u>that he may see</u>." And <u>the Lord opened the servant's eyes</u> <u>and he saw;</u> and behold, the mountain was full of horses and chariots of fire all around Elisha." 2 Kings 6:17

I believe it was the Lord's timing in my life that I learned this when I did, because shortly afterwards my mom passed away. I was heartbroken at first, of course.

On the Sunday after her funeral, during worship with my eyes closed, I asked the Lord to show me my mother and father in heaven. My dad had passed away many years before. Immediately, I saw my mom and dad in a beautiful garden. They were young, really young, like the ages they were before they had kids. Mom was sitting on a swing and dad handed her a single red rose. I could feel how completely carefree and happy they were! It was a wonderful vision and brought me so much comfort to know where my parents are, how carefree they are and that I'll be with them again one day.

Gary Oates also taught that once you go somewhere in a vision you can go back to that same place again. So, later on I closed my eyes and purposed to go back to that garden. This time mom and dad left the garden and walked down a path to a river, holding hands. Dad started fishing, which he always loved to do and mom reclined on the grass. I sat with mom and looked in wonder at her young face. I also saw myself in that vision. I looked like I was around 20 years old and had long hair down to my waist. Afterwards, I thought that this must have been a vision of the future and I stopped cutting my hair and let it grow long. I figured if it was good enough for heaven, it was good enough for earth.

I walked over to dad and we put our arms around each other. I laid my head on his shoulder and told him how much I missed him all these years. Then, my brother walked up holding a whole bunch of fish he had caught with a huge, happy smile on his face. We were all so joyful and carefree! Then, we walked up to a house with a huge outdoor entertaining space where the fish were cooked for dinner.

Suddenly, I wanted to paint a picture and thought "where will I get a canvas and paint"? First, I thought that I simply had to speak them into existence, but actually I simply thought it and they appeared. I started painting and looked around and started seeing that my whole family was there. There were my brothers, sisters, their kids, aunts, uncles, cousins, grandparents, great-grandparents, their brothers and sisters and so on. Some of these people I had never met, but somehow I knew who they were. It was a huge family gathering!

Suddenly, I saw God sitting on His throne. He spoke our family's last name in great power and the whole family came into existence.

We started playing soccer in a big field and I called to my Uncle Squire to come kick the soccer ball with us. He came running down the hill and began to play. I wept when I saw this, because he had had polio since he was a young child and was crippled all his life. Now, here he was running and playing and happy. I saw my son and grandson, who had both suffered injuries to their knees and ankles, now playing on strong, healed legs. The entire family was healed, whole and strong. I wept with joy!

Years earlier, I had been trying to do a family genealogy and had hit a dead end and become frustrated. The Lord said, "Your heritage is with Me." At those words, I let the whole thing go and just trusted Him with it. Now, after seeing my whole family in heaven, I understood what He meant!

All of the promises of God that we haven't appropriated here, we will there.

BACK TO THE GARDEN

Later on, I decided to go back again to that garden where I had seen my mom sitting on a swing and my dad handing her a single red rose. This time, I saw that it was me sitting on the swing and Jesus handed me a single red rose! What a beautiful picture of how Jesus loves us!

"Husbands, love your wives, even <u>as Christ also loved the church</u>, and gave himself for it." Ephesians 5: 25

"<u>Behold, thou art fair, my love</u>; behold, thou art fair; thou hast doves' eyes." Song of Solomon 1:15

"My beloved is mine, and I am his" Song of Solomon 2:16

"<u>Thou hast ravished my heart, my sister, my spouse</u>; thou hast ravished my heart with one of thine eyes, with one chain of thy neck. How fair is thy love, my sister, my spouse! how much better is thy love than wine! and the smell of thine ointments than all spices!

Thy lips, O my spouse, drop as the honeycomb: honey and milk are under thy tongue; and the smell of thy garments is like the smell of Lebanon.

<u>A garden enclosed is my sister, my spouse</u>; a spring shut up, a fountain sealed. A fountain of gardens, a well of living waters, and streams from Lebanon.

Awake, O north wind; and come, thou south; blow upon my garden, that the spices thereof may flow out. Let my beloved come into his garden, and eat his pleasant fruits." Song of Solomon 3:9-12, 15-16

"My beloved is gone down into his garden, to the beds of spices, to feed in the gardens, and to gather lilies." Song of Solomon 6:2

MARRIAGE SUPPER OF THE LAMB

Another time, I saw my family in heaven, seated at a long banquet table. I looked over at my son and he had the happiest look on his face that I've ever seen. Jesus said, "He's full of glory."

KEEP LOOKING

Gary Oates had also taught that when you begin to see something in the spirit, keep looking and you'll see more.

During worship, I saw God sitting on His throne, real blurry at first. I kept looking and saw that He was dressed all in white, with a gold belt and gold sash across His shoulder. I saw the bottom of His white, curly beard and I thought, "He doesn't shave". I kept looking and saw that His throne was solid gold with large, beautiful gems adorning it. I saw a gold crown on His head and noticed that His throne was lifted up very high. He is King, Ruler and Sovereign! I felt the spirit inside my heart pounding and very peaceful.

DANCING WITH JESUS

I went to a worship meeting at the house of some friends and while we were waiting for others to arrive, I looked out the window into the backyard and saw the strangest thing. It was raining very heavily on half the yard and there was no rain falling on the other half. Everyone came to the window to see and I felt in my spirit that God was causing that to get our attention. Then, suddenly a rainbow appeared in the backyard! The Lord said it was a sign of His pleasure that we were taking the time to gather to worship Him.

When worship began, Jesus came to me and we started dancing cheek to cheek. It was awesome! I felt so close to Him and could feel his wonderful love! He said, "Not much longer. I'm coming back for you. Don't lose heart/hope."

"Thou hast turned for me my mourning into dancing: thou hast put off my sackcloth, and girded me with gladness"
Psalm 30:11

DANCING WITH MY FATHER

One evening at home, the Spirit led me to worship. Then, He said, "I'm going to give you a new experience with me." I saw a gate and stepped through it. I saw my Father on His throne. He stood up and came to dance with me. Wow! We danced, He spun me, then He said, "Let Me lead", which made me laugh. He said, "I'll let you smell me"; it was a sweet and complex fragrance and smelled faintly like chocolate to me. He whispered in my ear, "I love you", over and over again. "My power will flow through you in a great way. You will see signs and miracles and healing will flow through your hands. Don't be afraid." (I laughed again, how well He knows me.) "Great multitudes will come into the kingdom through your words. I already see your future and all these things will come to pass. Now you get the pleasure of walking them out. That's it for now", then He spun me one last time and went and sat down. He said, "I don't always sit on the throne." (He gets up sometimes and does other things.)

DANCING IN HEAVEN

I went back to the place where I saw my family. This time, Jesus and I were walking down the path holding hands. I thought we were going to head up the hill to see the family, but Jesus said, "Wait, not yet." He led me to a field with the softest, greenest grass I'd ever seen and we danced barefoot together. It was wonderful!

YOU ARE GOD'S DIAMOND

Another time during worship at home, God and Jesus were each holding my hands.

The Lord said to me, "I've had you under a lot of pressure for a long time and I've turned you into a diamond. It's the strongest substance, it's the most beautiful substance and it's the most valuable substance."

Then, I was dancing before my Father. I was both me and I was a diamond with brilliant light flashing out. There were other people/diamonds, too. Each one was unique and dancing and spinning before the throne.

Then, I sat on my Father's lap like his little daughter and He kissed my cheek and said "You are not common, you're uncommon! I have you in the palm of my hand", and suddenly I was dancing on the palm of His hand!

"And they shall be mine, saith the LORD of hosts, in that day when I make up my jewels; and I will spare them, as a man spareth his own son that serveth him." Malachi 3:17

DANCE PARTY IN HEAVEN

In heaven, I saw my old friend from high school, Robbie, who had committed suicide when he was a teenager. Somehow I knew that his twin brother was there also, although I didn't see him. He had lunged at police with a knife on the one year anniversary of his brother's suicide so that they would shoot him. Robbie and I hugged and danced, Jesus joined in and the 3 of us did a circle dance. We were absolutely filled with the love of Jesus!

There were multitudes around us, all dancing joyously! I saw another old friend of mine and we danced. There was nothing but love, joy and harmony between all of us. "You have friends here, real friends," the Lord said. Wonderful!

Then, in unison all the dancing people said to me, "Its okay!

You're on your way here!" I knew this present life with all its troubles is for some purpose and it won't last. We'll be there forever, having a dance party!

"Rejoice ye in that day, and leap for joy: for, behold, your reward is great in heaven." Luke 6:23

"With gladness and rejoicing shall they be brought: they shall enter into the king's palace." Psalm 45:15

THE GOLD OF HEAVEN IN GOD'S TREASURY

In Gary Oates book, he tells about a woman who went to God's throne where He gave her a gold coin and told her to swallow it. He said, "This is the gold of heaven."

When I read that, I asked Him, "What is the gold of heaven?" The Lord said, "Pray in the spirit", then, "I'm giving you the key to heaven. With it you'll be able to unlock mysteries." An angel put a large, solid gold key in my outstretched hands. Then, I used the key to unlock a box in heaven. It was full of gold coins.

"This is my treasury," said the Lord. I looked around the room, which was so large that I couldn't see any walls and it was full of huge piles of gold coins and some other gold objects in the distance that I couldn't clearly see. Wow! I didn't even know He had a treasury!

"I lead in the way of righteousness, in the midst of the paths of judgment: That I may cause those that love me to inherit substance; and I will fill their treasures." Proverbs 8: 20-21

"In the house of the righteous is much treasure: but in the revenues of the wicked is trouble." Proverbs 15:6

"Lay not up for yourselves treasures upon earth, where moth

and rust doth corrupt, and where thieves break through and steal: But <u>lay up for yourselves treasures in heaven</u>, where neither moth nor rust doth corrupt, and where thieves do not break through nor steal: For where your treasure is, there will your heart be also." Matthew 6: 19-21

"Now when Jesus heard these things, he said unto him, Yet lackest thou one thing: sell all that thou hast, and distribute unto the poor, <u>and thou shalt have treasure in heaven</u>: and come, follow me." Luke 18:22

AN ANGEL NAMED BREAKTHROUGH

Another time, He drew me to worship. I became aware that worshipping angels were present. Then, He sent an angel whose <u>name is Breakthrough</u>! Wow! This made me wonder about the possible names of other angels. Healing? Joy? Peace? Love?

HE IS LIGHT

During worship, the singer started singing a song called *He is Light*. Suddenly, I saw Jesus high and lifted up. He was dressed in a garment covered with embedded diamonds and brilliant light was shining out from Him! Beautiful!

"Then spake Jesus again unto them, saying, <u>I am the light of the world</u>: he that followeth me shall not walk in darkness, but shall have the light of life." John 8:12

SEATED TOGETHER WITH HIM IN HEAVENLY PLACES

I saw Jesus high above me, sitting on His throne. He reached His hand down, took my hand and lifted me up with Him and seated me on a throne beside Him.

"But God, who is rich in mercy, for his great love wherewith he loved us, even when we were dead in sins, hath quickened us together with Christ, (by grace ye are saved;) and hath raised us up together, and made us sit together in heavenly places in Christ Jesus; that in the ages to come he might show the exceeding riches of his grace in his kindness toward us through Christ Jesus." Ephesians 2: 4-7

RULE AND REIGN WITH HIM

Another time, I saw Jesus sitting on His throne with a golden glow all around it. I was in awe for a while. Then, He motioned for me to sit beside Him. I sat down and a crown was put on my head. He reached His left hand over and held my hand. I noticed that He was wearing a ring, but I couldn't clearly see the detail of it. I was overwhelmed by, "He took the initiative." He said, "Now, rule and reign with Me."

"Blessed is the man that endureth temptation: for when he is tried, he shall receive the crown of life, which the Lord hath promised to them that love him." James 1:12

"If we suffer, we shall also reign with him: if we deny him, he also will deny us." 2 Timothy 2:12

"And hast made us unto our God kings and priests: and we shall reign on the earth." Revelation 5:10

I GO TO PREPARE A PLACE FOR YOU

Another time in worship, the Lord said I'm going to show you something – wait... I saw Jesus standing next to an empty throne. He gestured toward it and said, "This is your place, this is your place, this is where you belong. This is the place I've prepared for you. Enter into your reward. You'll rule and reign with me forever." (I thought of all the difficulties of life and the reward well worth it.)

"In my Father's house are many mansions: if it were not so, I would have told you. I go to prepare a place for you." John 14:2

SPEAK HIS WORD

Another time, He said, "Take your place on this throne", and I sat down. "Now rule and reign with Me." "How, Lord?" I asked. "What you hear me say, speak it out of your mouth. My words must come to pass. It's already written. Multitudes of souls will come into the kingdom through God's Word spoken by you."

"For verily I say unto you, That whosoever shall say unto this mountain, Be thou removed, and be thou cast into the sea; and shall not doubt in his heart, but shall believe that those things which he saith shall come to pass; he shall have whatsoever he saith." Mark 11:23

THIS IS GOING TO BE FUN

Another time, I saw Jesus motioning to my empty throne. "Come and take your place beside me", He said. We both sat down and He looked over at me and said, "This is going to be fun!" The saints of God are privileged!

The Lord said, "Only a few more steps to take in this world, then you'll be with Me forever."

ALL OF CREATION LOVES JESUS

I saw Jesus snow skiing down a mountain! Afterwards, in a ski lodge, He sat on the hearth in front of the fire. Me and a group of others sat facing him and listened to Him talk about, surprisingly, skiing! A rabbit hopped up to him. Jesus had a beautiful relationship with him and the rabbit loved being in His presence.

Another time, Jesus came to me and took my hand. We went walking up a hill together. We saw deer, rabbits and birds and none of them were afraid of us! At the top of the hill, Jesus stretched out his arm to show me the most beautiful view.

"And it shall come to pass, that before they call, I will answer; and while they are yet speaking, I will hear. The wolf and the lamb shall feed together, and the lion shall eat straw like the bullock: and dust shall be the serpent's meat. They shall not hurt nor destroy in all my holy mountain, saith the LORD." Isaiah 65:24-25

I saw dogs in heaven, playing on the side of a hill. All sizes and breeds were playing together happily. I kept looking and saw a stream at the bottom of the hill. The dogs ran down and drank and splashed around. I kept looking and saw an angel at the top of the other hill who whistled and called to the dogs. They all ran up and the angel fed them, and then put them in a barn for the night. They lay down happily on sweet smelling hay. Outside, two other angels stood having a leisurely conversation with the first angel. He was the Keeper of the Dogs.

I saw my own dogs in heaven. First I saw the dogs I currently own, later I saw the dogs I had growing up. They were really young and so happy!

SNOOP DOG

Our dear dog, Snoop, got cancer when he was 13 years old. Surgery wasn't recommended and we did all we could to take care of him until it came to a point where he was in constant pain and we knew it was best for him to have him put to sleep. The vet came to the house on my birthday since we couldn't transport him and he went peacefully.

Later, when I saw him in heaven, he was young, strong and very happy. I went to visit many times and learned that you can interact in that heavenly realm. The Lord said, "You can come here whenever you want to."

I was in a big field and I called to Snoop who came running up very happy to see me. I petted his soft head and he turned around so I could scratch his back which was always his favorite spot. The Lord told me, "He's happy when you come, but he isn't sad when you go."

BE FRUITFUL AND MULTIPLY

Another time, I saw Snoop with a litter of his puppies. He was being really tender with them and then taking them down to the river to learn to swim. Precious!

THE BAD TIMES WILL CEASE TO EXIST

Once, I was remembering a really nice time in my life and I felt sad that it was over. Suddenly, the Lord said to me, "In the ages to come, the good times will exist forever; the bad times will cease to exist."

JESUS LAUGHING

During worship in church, I saw Jesus sitting on His throne holding His scepter. He was looking out at all the worshippers and then He started laughing with joy! He was so joyful to be with His family!

KING OF KINGS

During worship, I saw in the spirit, King Jesus on the platform sitting on His throne, with a gold crown on his head, a gold scepter in his hand and dressed in royal garments. I stood in awe of the King for quite awhile. Then He said, "Look at yourself."

I looked down and saw that I was also dressed in royal garments and had a gold crown on my head. Then, I looked up and saw that the entire congregation of worshippers were wearing royal garments with gold crowns on their heads. He is the King of kings and we are His kings!

"And I put a jewel on thy forehead, and earrings in thine ears, and <u>a beautiful crown upon thine head</u>." Ezekiel 16:2

THE FIRE OF GOD

One Sunday, the associate pastor was preaching. Suddenly, in the spirit, I saw a flame of fire shooting out of his mouth! As I watched in amazement, he started gesturing with his hands as he talked and I saw flames of fire shooting out of both hands! Afterwards, I told him what I had seen. He said that was a great encouragement to him as he was just getting ready to travel to Uganda on a missionary trip and felt that the fire of God was going with him to minister to the people there. God is so good!

"And of the angels he saith, Who maketh his angels spirits, and <u>his ministers a flame of fire</u>." Hebrews 1:7

RIVER OF GOD

I was floating on my back on a crystal clear river totally carefree. I looked over to my left and saw Jesus floating on his back beside me. He took my hand as we floated down the river together and He said, "This is the life!"

"And he showed me a pure <u>river of water of life</u>, clear as crystal, proceeding out of the throne of God and of the Lamb." Revelation 22:1

BEINGS OF LIGHT

I came to church early one day and sat watching the musicians practice worship songs. Suddenly I saw all 5 of them as beings of light! I saw the outlines of their bodies, but instead of flesh they were light! They were moving around, gesturing with their arms and they were made of light.

"<u>Ye are the light of the world</u>. A city that is set on a hill cannot be hid." Matthew 4:15

"<u>Let your light so shine before men</u>, that they may see your good works, and glorify your Father which is in heaven." Matthew 5:16

"Take heed therefore that <u>the light which is in thee</u> be not darkness.

<u>If thy whole body therefore be full of light, having no part dark, the whole shall be full of light, as when the bright shining of a candle doth give thee light</u>." Luke 11: 35-36

MINISTRY OF ANGELS

During worship, I saw my friend kneeling at the altar. The pastor came over to pray for her and said that God was anointing her with oil. Suddenly, in the spirit, I saw a 10 foot tall angel standing next to her! He was holding a huge pitcher full of oil and he was pouring it all over her!

THE LOVE OF THE FATHER

During a very difficult time in my life I spent a lot of time simply sitting on God's lap. He comforted me and filled me with His love there. Once, He kissed me on the top of my head! What a beautiful picture of His tender love toward us!

"Behold, <u>what manner of love the Father hath bestowed upon us</u>, that we should be called the sons of God: therefore the world knoweth us not, because it knew him not." 1 John 3:1

"And hope maketh not ashamed; because <u>the love of God is shed abroad in our hearts by the Holy Ghost</u> which is given unto us." Romans 5:5

"<u>Nor height, nor depth, nor any other creature, shall be able to separate us from the love of God, which is in Christ Jesus our Lord.</u>" Romans 8:39

Here's my prayer for you:

Father, open the eyes of the reader of this book and let them see into the spiritual realm like never before, in Jesus name. Amen.

CHAPTER 7

I WANT YOU THERE, PRAYING FOR PEOPLE

I was driving home from church one Sunday when the Lord directed me to pull into the parking lot of another church along the way. At first, I wasn't sure why. Then he directed my attention to the building next door which was one of those pay by the week, efficiency hotels. He said, "I want you there, praying for people." I said, "Okay Lord, but I need a partner. I don't want to go there alone."

The following weekend I went on a Saturday soul winning outreach. The group leader was talking about his strategy and discussing possible new areas to go to. I said that I felt the Lord calling me to the budget hotel. He was surprised and said, "You're kidding! Brian and Stephanie just told me the same thing."

So, the Lord teamed us up and we started doing outreach to the budget hotel. He gave us the grace to minister to and pray for a lot of people there over the next 2 years. We mostly went door to door offering to pray for people. We saw salvations, healings and many answers to prayer for jobs, finances, families, etc.

One day I was standing out front in the parking lot when a lady and her 6 children came walking by. The kids were probably from 4 to 16 years old. I shared the gospel with them and the whole family prayed to receive Jesus!

Once, my partner and I came across a young man in his mid-twenties, sitting in the stair well. We began to minister to him and pray over him. He didn't engage with us and didn't answer when we asked for his name, but he also didn't tell us to go away. He looked extremely troubled and in my spirit I felt that someone had done him wrong and he was contemplating taking revenge. Finally I said, "In Jesus name, everything that's not of God leave him now!" Immediately, it was as if a dark cloud over him disappeared. He looked at me and in a very vulnerable voice said, "My name is Joe." We were then able to minister the love of God to him.

Another Saturday we were at the budget hotel and a woman walked up to us and asked for prayer. She said she didn't live at that hotel, but that morning in prayer the Lord told her to go there. She had emphysema and every breath she took was short and labored. We laid our hands on her and prayed and one of the women in our group said she felt the power of the Holy Spirit go through her hands into the woman's chest. Then, Brian told her to take a deep breath. She breathed in and out normally a couple of times and broke into tears, saying "I'm healed! I'm healed." The emphysema was gone!

"And these signs shall follow them that believe; In my name shall they cast out devils; they shall speak with new tongues;

They shall take up serpents; and if they drink any deadly thing, it shall not hurt them; they shall lay hands on the sick, and they shall recover." Mark 16:17-18

CHAPTER 8

HOW GREAT IS OUR GOD

I was watching Rodney Howard-Browne videos and got really full of the spirit. When the video was over, I turned it off and this prayer just came out of my spirit, "Lord, reveal yourself to me in a way that I don't know you yet." I lay down to go to sleep and immediately I saw in the spirit that I was standing in front of God's throne. All around were a multitude of angels singing praises to God. The sound was so beautiful! They were singing, "How great is our God, sing with me, how great is our God, all will see how great, how great, is our God. You're the name above all names, you are worthy of all praise, and my heart will sing how great is our God."

This went on for quite awhile, and then the singing stopped. As I looked, Father God stood up from His throne. He began to become transparent. Now, instead of looking at His image, I saw a large ball of bright, white light. Out of this light, smaller bolts of light were streaking out and shooting off in different directions. This scripture came up in my spirit,

"Out of the throne proceeded lightnings." I began to weep. I wasn't sad, I was just weeping, overcome by how great God is. It was as if my useless body lay weeping on my bed while the real me was standing before God.

After awhile, the light changed and now I was looking at a powerful ball of swirling energy. I could feel it and thought, this is the most powerful energy in the universe. It was awesome and I continued to weep. After awhile, God became visible again. He sat down and asked me a question, "Do you believe that I can do anything?" My strange reply was, "You are everything! You are everything!"

Next I was looking at the fabric of His garment up close. It was absolutely the most beautiful thing that I've ever seen. I was searching for adjectives to adequately describe it, but couldn't find any. I was mesmerized by it and felt like I would be content to spend the rest of eternity simply gazing at that fabric. As I watched, the fabric began to become transparent. Now instead of seeing fabric, I was looking at what I knew to be the entire universe. I saw stars, planets and spiral galaxies. I had the realization that God wraps himself in the entire universe. After awhile, the fabric became visible again.

I looked over to my right and saw Jesus standing with a gold crown on his head and dressed in a royal cape down to His feet. I was stunned to my core and first thought, He is Splendor! Then it hit me even more profoundly, and I thought, He is Majesty! Not just He is majestic, but He is Majesty! King of kings and Lord of lords!

Finally, I looked back to the Father. He stretched out his hand, palm up and I looked into His hand close up. I could see people, what I knew to be billions and billions of people and I was struck by the thought that He knew each one of them on an individual basis. I cried out, how is that possible? How is that possible? What kind of being are you? How great! How great is our God!

I was overwhelmed by the realization that after seeing God this way, I would never be the same again.

"Bless the Lord, O my soul. O Lord my God, thou art very great; thou art clothed with honour and majesty.

Who coverest thyself with light as with a garment: who stretchest out the heavens like a curtain:

Who layeth the beams of his chambers in the waters: who maketh the clouds his chariot: who walketh upon the wings of the wind:" Psalm 104:1-3

"When I consider thy heavens, the work of thy fingers, the moon and the stars, which thou hast ordained;

What is man, that thou art mindful of him? and the son of man, that thou visitest him?" Psalm 8:3-4

"And out of the throne proceeded lightnings and thunderings and voices: and there were seven lamps of fire burning before the throne, which are the seven Spirits of God". Revelation 4:5

CHAPTER 9

TRANSLATION BY FAITH

When I was first saved, I had a vision where I knew I was "traveling for the Lord". I was flying (I assumed I was in a plane) and I looked over to my left and saw tall, skinny mountains like you see in the Orient. I held onto that vision for many years.

I first heard the teaching about translation by faith by Bruce D. Allen on the Sid Roth It's Supernatural TV show. *I was very intrigued by it.*

He was talking about how we can be supernaturally transported from one place to another and that this is for every believer.

This is what happened to Philip the evangelist after he baptized the eunuch as recorded in the book of Acts, chapter 8:

"And as they went on their way, they came unto a certain water: and the eunuch said, See, here is water; what doth hinder me to be baptized? And Philip said, If thou believest

with all thine heart, thou mayest. And he answered and said, I believe that Jesus Christ is the Son of God.

And he commanded the chariot to stand still: and they went down both into the water, both Philip and the eunuch; and he baptized him. And when they were come up out of the water, <u>the Spirit of the Lord caught away Philip,</u> that the eunuch saw him no more: and he went on his way rejoicing. But Philip was found at Azotus: and passing through he preached in all the cities, till he came to Caesarea."

The Spirit of the Lord caught Philip away to the town of Azotus, about 30 miles away.

Again, this is what happened when Jesus entered into the boat with the disciples:

"But he said to them, "It is I; don't be afraid." Then they were willing to take him into the boat, and <u>immediately the boat reached the shore where they were heading.</u>" John 6:20-21 NIV

This is also what happened to Enoch when the Spirit of the Lord caught him away:

"<u>By faith Enoch was translated</u> that he should not see death; and was not found, because God had translated him: for before his translation he had this testimony, that he pleased God." Hebrews 11:5

I had an experience in the spirit where Jesus came and took me by the hand and we went flying. I was aware of a multitude of angels flying with us. I looked over to my left and saw those tall, narrow mountains! We landed on a platform in front of a very large group of people. Jesus put his arm around my shoulders and spoke into my ear the words to say to the people. Part of what He said was, "Tell them that I love them. Tell them that I died for their sins. Invite them to come forward to receive me." I shared the words of Jesus with them and then invited them to come forward to pray a prayer of salvation. A large crowd of people came forward and received Jesus.

It was awesome that the vision I had years ago of travelling for the Lord and seeing those tall, narrow mountains had come to pass in this unexpected, supernatural way. God is so amazing! He can do anything!

"He bowed the heavens also, and came down; and darkness was under his feet. And he rode upon a cherub, and did fly: and he was seen upon the wings of the wind." 2 Samuel 22:10-12

Another time, Jesus came to me, took me by the hand and we went flying in the spirit. We landed on a platform in front of a multitude of people. Again, Jesus put His arm around my shoulders and spoke into my ear the words to say to the people. This time, there was another man on the platform with us who translated the words of Jesus that I spoke. While we were speaking, people began to throw down their crutches and get out of their wheel chairs and walk! Healing broke out throughout the crowd. Then, Jesus told me to call the people forward to receive Him and a huge number of people gave their hearts to Him. It was awesome!

I had another translation experience in the spirit where I was taken to the side of a lake. There was a young man lying on the ground with 4 or 5 people standing around him. I looked down at his leg and saw that he had an enormous gash in it. A huge hunk of flesh was hanging off and it was bleeding profusely. I simply reached out and touched his leg and it was restored to normal. I didn't say a word or even have a single thought. Then we were gone.

One thing I've noticed during translation experiences in the spirit is how pure the ministry is. There is no reasoning involved, no wondering what to say or do; it's simply saying what Jesus says and being a vessel that the Holy Spirit flows through.

Here's my prayer for you:

Father, bless the reader of this book and activate them to be supernaturally transported by faith to accomplish Your will, in Jesus name. Amen.

CHAPTER 10

SEEDTIME AND HARVEST

I was on a Saturday outreach with a group of people at the town square where they were having a festival. The Lord told me to go over to a certain booth to talk to the people there. When I got there, I discovered that the booth was the Samaritan's Purse Operation Christmas Child (OCC) people. I prayed with them and gave them my contact information.

Three years later, a lady from a bank where I didn't have an account called me to say that if I would come into the branch and open a checking account and do at least one direct deposit, they would give me a $250 sign on bonus. I said, Yes!

The next day I got an email from a prayer leader with Samaritan's Purse OCC inviting me to attend a prayer meeting at her house. My spirit leapt inside me and I knew to go. There were about 10 to 12 people there and we were also on a conference call with multiple other prayer groups.

When it came time for me to pray, the spirit of God just prayed through me. It was really powerful and I've never experienced prayer like that before.

They were telling us about OCC, where you buy small toys, put them into a shoebox and bring them to their distribution center where they add a Gospel book to it and ship them to children all over the world for Christmas.

I felt strongly impressed to make 10 boxes and let the leader know that. When I got home and visited their website for more details, I saw that each box costs $25 to make. That would cost me $250, the exact amount of my bank bonus! God provided in advance!

So, I assembled 10 boxes and printed the labels to go with them. The labels have a tracking number so you can go on the website later to see where your boxes were shipped. It was maybe a month later that I checked the website and saw that my boxes had been shipped to children in Congo.

Now months later during a church service, the pastor called me by name to come forward for prayer. He said he was being obedient to the Spirit and that the Lord had showed him something that day while he was in prayer. As I walked to the front the spirit came on me so strong that I began to cry and could hardly walk straight. He said, the Lord is calling you to a people group that you haven't considered and He's crowning you with the anointing for that. He laid his hand on my head and I fell down backward under the power of God and wept on the floor.

Later that night, I had an experience with God where I was translated in the spirit to another location. Jesus came to me, took me by the hand and we went flying. We landed in a small village where the curious people gathered around us. Jesus spoke into my ear the words to say to these villagers.

Somehow I spoke in their language a gospel message, and then gave an invitation for them to receive Jesus. They prayed a prayer inviting Him into their hearts and then the Holy Spirit filled them and they began speaking in a heavenly language. It was awesome!

Then, Jesus and I travelled to another village. I wasn't aware of a journey; we were simply at another village instantly. Again, Jesus spoke into my ear the words to say and these villagers also received Jesus and the Spirit. We continued going from village to village, some were small; others were large with a bigger population – all night long. At the end of the night, I heard a number. It was 850,000. I wasn't asking and wasn't even wondering about how many people had been won to Christ that night. I simply heard the number. It reminded me of what John wrote in the book of Revelation where he heard a number.

"And I heard the number of them which were sealed: and there were sealed an hundred and forty and four thousand of all the tribes of the children of Israel." Revelation 7:4

"And the number of the army of the horsemen were two hundred thousand thousand: and I heard the number of them." Revelation 9:16

The next day I was praying about all of this and I asked the Lord where we had gone. He said it was the Heart of Africa. I Googled Heart of Africa and was astounded to see that it is Congo!

He had started setting this up 3 years earlier when He connected me with the OCC people, then led me to make 10 Christmas boxes with money He provided in advance, then had those boxes sent to Congo, then took me to Congo to preach the gospel! I simply planted the seed He had provided and He reaped a harvest! He is amazing!

Shortly afterwards I had another experience where I was translated in the spirit to Nairobi, Kenya. I came face to face with a young, black man out on the dusty street. He was wearing medium blue colored work pants, black leather shoes and a white collared shirt and was covered with the dust from the street. Jesus was standing next to me and told me what to say to this man. I did and he gave his heart to Jesus in prayer. The Lord said to me, "I come for the one." This made me think that it isn't about numbers, it's about simply being obedient to what God wants to do.

THE AGES TO COME

My father took me in an instant to the very edge of the universe, to the very last star. We looked out into … space. He said, "It's empty right now."

Right now…Right now? As if it won't always be empty?

Okay, this is speculation on my part, but what if, in the ages to come, we, being made in His image, with the same creative ability in our words, being imitators of our dear Father, will speak into existence a new universe into that empty right now space? What if that's part of His plan for the ages to come?

What do you think he means by, "Empty right now?"

"But as it is written, Eye hath not seen, nor ear heard, neither have entered into the heart of man, the things which God hath prepared for them that love him. But God hath revealed them unto us by his Spirit: for the Spirit searcheth all things, yea, the deep things of God." 1 Corinthians 2:9-10